"John Wooden is an American treasure whose stunning achievements are singular but whose message is universal: hard work, integrity, and love of family are at the core of living a good life. *The Wisdom of Wooden* shares a lifetime's worth of people, places, and ideas that shaped the greatest coach of the twentieth century. John Wooden continues to amaze, inspire, and inform millions of admirers around the world."

—DR. STEPHEN COVEY, Author and Speaker

"Throughout his long and legendary life, Coach John Wooden has demonstrated that excellence at the highest level in the most competitive arenas can be achieved and sustained by doing it 'the right way,' namely, with integrity, fidelity, and honor—qualities he also personified as a husband and father. *The Wisdom of Wooden* is his wonderful tribute to those who helped him on his life's journey."

—JOHN C. MAXWELL, Author and Speaker

"As a legendary coach and as the chairman of the McDonald's All-American Games, Coach John Wooden's influential wisdom has taught players that what they do off the court is just as important as what they do on the court. No one and no player cares more about the game of basketball or the players than Coach Wooden."

—JIM SKINNER, CEO, McDonald's Corporation

"His stories are enchanting; his wisdom is profound. I believe you will become a John Wooden disciple, as I am, when you read *The Wisdom of Wooden.*"

—KEN BLANCHARD,
coauthor of *The One Minute Manager*®

"Coach John Wooden is a hero to many of us because he represents a way of living life and doing your job that reflects America at its very best. *The Wisdom of Wooden* shares the principles and priorities, people and places that have guided him throughout his amazing life for almost a century. It should come as no surprise that his guidance and example are more important today than ever before."

—JIM SINEGAL, CEO, Costco

"Though we call John Wooden 'Coach,' he is a teacher at heart, a teacher whose classroom in life was a court. The lessons he taught were about living honestly and generously, and about becoming the best you can be. While he coached only his players, his book teaches us all. We're lucky that we have a window into his timeless principles and unmatched wisdom."

—JUDY OLIAN, Dean and John E. Anderson Chair,
UCLA Anderson School of Management

"[A]n incredible coach, and an even better man . . . As a basketball fan, I remember fondly his ten NCAA championships, his unrivaled winning streak at UCLA, and the caliber of players he mentored. But as an American, I salute the way he achieved all that success—with modesty, and humility, and by wholeheartedly dedicating his life to the betterment of others. Even after he became one of the game's early heroes, he worked as a high school teacher. And for the rest of his life, on and off the court, he never stopped teaching. He never stopped preparing his players, and everyone he met, to be their best."

—PRESIDENT BARACK OBAMA

"Although he is Coach John Wooden to America, he is Daddy to me—my father, whom I love very much. I am so proud that his example of how to live life—both personally and professionally—has been important to so many for so long. *The Wisdom of Wooden* is his thank you to everyone—the most personal and revealing description he's ever offered about his life. You'll laugh, learn, and, at times, you may notice a tear coming down your cheek. *The Wisdom of Wooden* is the best book you'll ever read about my dad."

—NAN MUEHLHAUSEN WOODEN, Coach Wooden's Daughter

"What an amazing life. But here's what's even more amazing about John Wooden and the timeless verities his life has embodied. One hundred years from now they will still be talking about his accomplishments and his approach."

—BOB COSTAS, Broadcaster

"John Wooden is a philosopher-coach, a man whose beliefs, teachings, and wisdom go far beyond sports, and ultimately address how to bring out the very best in yourself and others in all areas of life."

—BILL WALSH, San Francisco 49ers

"Other than my own father, he is the wisest man I've ever known. To rub shoulders with his perpetual pursuit of excellence and goodness was to be motivated to strive for the best one could become. The bar will never be set higher. His consciousness and commitment to what is right carries a precious life lesson for all whom he touched. By any measurement, Coach Wooden will always be the greatest coach/teacher/counselor in the history of his sport—perhaps any sport. John Wooden? Oh my!"

—DICK ENBERG, Broadcaster

The Wisdom of Wooden is a powerful message from my father about his life's journey and what you might learn from it. Dad's compass in my own life has been true and constant in all areas. What he taught me I taught my children. Nevertheless, for many years I didn't grasp the extent of his positive influence on other people. When it gradually dawned on me many years ago, it was stunning and gratifying. I can't think of a better way to know about my dad than *The Wisdom of Wooden*."

—JIM WOODEN, Coach Wooden's Son

"John Wooden is the greatest coach in the history of team sports, but his success on the bench is dwarfed by his achievements away from the basketball court. As a coach, he was an intense competitor and the consummate champion. John Wooden the man has strong moral principles, an innate kindness, a gift for treating everyone with dignity, and the strength to always adhere to his core beliefs. He was given a forum by God to speak of the things that are important in his life, and he has used that forum to enrich the lives of millions of others through his strength, enthusiasm, honesty, intelligence, and humility. He sets an example for all of us by constantly striving to be the best in every aspect of his life. Throughout my life, I have found inspiration and direction in the Bible. Today, I also find inspiration and direction in the words of John Wooden."

—TOM COUGHLIN, Head Coach, New York Giants

"John Wooden is a monument to 'how to'—how to approach and embrace the spirit of competition; how to prepare; how to lead; how to win and, on those rare occasions, lose with dignity, grace, and class."

—GREG GUMBEL, CBS Sports

2 3 4 5 6 7 LPR 1 5 4 3 2 1

ISBN: 978-0-07-175116-2
MHID: 0-07-175116-5

Book design by Tom Lau

Photographs are from the authors' personal collections unless otherwise indicated. Other photos courtesy of Associated Press, ASUCLA, Tom Cassalini, Indiana State University, *Sports Illustrated*/Getty Images, *Los Angeles Times*, Purdue University, The Queens Borough Public Library—*New York Herald Tribune* Collection, *South Bend Tribune*.

ASUCLA Photography

THE WISDOM OF WOODEN

My Century On and Off the Court

Coach John Wooden
and Steve Jamison

New York   Chicago   San Francisco   Lisbon   London   Madrid   Mexico City
Milan   New Delhi   San Juan   Seoul   Singapore   Sydney   Toronto

To my wife, Nellie, who has been "my life" all my life and without whose patience, faith, understanding and love, I would be lost.

As ever and forever,

John

For Mom and Dad,

Steve

Special thanks to Nan Muehlhausen Wooden and Jim Wooden.

The authors would also like to thank Philip Ruppel, Ron Martirano, Tom Lau, Judith McCarthy, Ruth Mannino, Peter McCurdy, Gary Krebs, Roger Kasunic at McGraw-Hill; UCLA and Director of Athletics, Dan Guerrero; Dean Judy Olian and the UCLA Anderson School of Business/John Wooden Global Leadership Program, along with everyone else at UCLA for their years of support and friendship; Jill Hisey, Linds Foster, John Flokstra and School Specialty; Jim Powers, Eddie Powers, Elmer Reynolds; Steve Keay and his team at Perfection Learning, including Sue Theis, Randy Messer, Sue Conelison, Tobi Cunningham, and Jane Wonderlin; Bill Whitman and McDonald's All-American High School Basketball Games; Gary Cunningham, Denny Crum, Jerry Norman, Julie Gilman, Renee Broadwell, Deborah Morales, Karen Paulsell, Tony Spino, Ev and Harold Edstrom's Hal Leonard Publishing (plus Rog Busdicker); UCLA's Bill Bennett, Doug Erickson, Dennis Koehne, Dion Veloz; Boris and Sophia and The Valley Inn; Paul and Lucy and VIP's Café; Yoon Ju and Fromin's Restaurant; Mary's Place with Steve, Pat, KRS, Kate and Kim Edstrom; Peanut Louie Harper and ITP Design for their assistance on the Pyramid of Success illustrations; and a tip of the cap to Ev who was there when it all began.

"Coach Wooden," I asked respectfully, "how does it feel—100 years?" We were sitting in his small cluttered den (*neatly* cluttered, I should add) in Encino, California, surrounded by memorabilia. His one-hundredth birthday was fast approaching. With a small smile, Coach offered a brief answer: "More aches and pains, that's for sure. Art Linkletter said old age is no place for sissies." He chuckled and shook his head knowingly.

"But looking back," I continued, "what do you see? What can you tell me about all those years?" Slowly, he began talking, and as he talked, he began pointing—over here, over there—at some of the objects and photographs packed into his den. Thus began a memorable tour of the family, faith, and friends in this man's full and productive span, one in which he emerged as among the greatest coaches America has ever produced—perhaps the greatest.

The tour that afternoon was the genesis for *The Wisdom of Wooden*. As Coach talked, the memories pulled him back into a time of fewer aches and pains, a time when many of the people he loved and learned from were still with him in life rather than in pictures on the wall.

Above his old roll-top desk he pointed to a framed copy of a poem he loves, "A Little Fellow Follows Me"; on the desk, his Bible ("It's not there for decoration," he noted); next to it a photograph of his venerated coach at Purdue University, "Piggy" Lambert; amidst hundreds of books on the shelves, including poetry, biographies, and Shakespeare,

photos of family—his mother, Roxie Anna, his father, Joshua Hugh Wooden, his dear wife, Nell (including one of his favorite pictures of them as high schoolers); and, of course, a blizzard of snapshots of their children and grand-children and great-grandchildren. And along the way he offered keen observations on what he learned and whom he learned it from, including specifics on the evolution of his radical definition of success and the resultant and powerful Pyramid of Success—even more relevant today than when he created it.

"Over there," he said, looking at the wall above his tele-vision, "is the pyramid Nellie designed. I haven't changed it since she put it up thirty-five years ago with pictures of all ten teams that won a championship."

Later I realized those old 8 × 10 pictures were virtually the only evidence in the entire condo of his fabled dynasty—the UCLA basketball teams that had won ten national championships (seven of them in consecutive years!), eighty-eight straight games, four perfect seasons, and so on—or of his being crowned Greatest Coach of the Twentieth Century in various polls and awarded the Presidential Medal of Freedom in ceremonies at the White House.

At some point *Sports Illustrated* concluded: "There has never been a finer coach in American sports. Nor a finer man." It's that last part—"nor a finer man"—that makes John Wooden *JOHN WOODEN*.

—STEVE JAMISON

A Wise Man. When He Spoke, I Listened.

Wisdom is often in the eye of the beholder. What is profound for one may be less so for another; meaningful for me may be meaningless for you. For example, Joshua Hugh Wooden, my father, told me over and over that "nothing is stronger than gentleness." I came to see how true and powerful this is.

Nevertheless, I know from my own experience in sharing this idea with others that some relate to it; others just roll their eyes. That's all right. I, too, have rolled my eyes occasionally in the face of wisdom; we're only human. However, I'm pleased to say that I had sense enough never to roll my eyes when my father said something. When he spoke, I listened.

This book is from a lifetime's living and learning—a century. For some, the observations and information within may be useful; for others, not so much. You may find common sense within these pages or make no sense of it at all. Wisdom? I know my dad was wise. When I quote him, I am conveying what I believe is wisdom. When I branch out with my own ideas, you can decide for yourself what it is.

For this book, my longtime friend and collaborator, Steve Jamison, gathered photographs going back one hundred years, including many that he took during the considerable time we've known each other. I've added my reflections to them.

At the top of the list of things I hope our book conveys is the great amount of love that has filled my life—family first (Nellie, my dear wife and sweetheart, and Nan and Jim, our son and daughter; and the grandchildren, great-grandchildren, and coming up—a great-great-grandchild and hopefully many more) and then my extended family—those I taught and worked with (students, student-athletes, coaches, trainers, managers, teachers, athletic directors, principals, and chancellors), friends, acquaintances, and more and more these days complete strangers who come up and say, "Hi, Coach Wooden. We love you."

Love is the greatest word in the English dictionary. What joy it brings. We should all say it more often to those we love. Don't be shy about it!

I also hope our book shares in a meaningful manner the fundamental principles I've used in teaching and coaching and living my life. And, of course, faith is and has been so important to me and is present within these pages.

One hundred years. That's a long time. I personally don't know anybody older than me, so let me share something you can't possible comprehend as well as I do—at least not until you get to be my age: Life goes by in a flicker, and then you're gone. We are all pilgrims passing through on our way to eternity.

From the earliest age I learned from my dear mother, Roxie Anna, and father that time is precious and absolutely irreplaceable; each day matters. You only get this one blessed opportunity to make the effort to do your best. And then it's over. No second chance. The Good Lord judges you on what you've done and who you've been.

Thus, if I may offer you one piece of advice that I hope you'll apply after reading our book, it is this suggestion from my father: "Make *each* day your masterpiece." When you do that as the weeks and months and years (and, for me, century) unfold behind you, you'll have the deepest self-satisfaction knowing your life has really meant something. You will have achieved the most important kind of success, namely, becoming the best that you are capable of becoming. It is impossible to accomplish more than that. My father taught me this, and it has been at the center of my thinking since the day I left home and went out on my own.

—JOHN WOODEN

Dad believed everyone should have a philosophy of life if you were to amount to anything. When I graduated from a small country grade school in Centerton, Indiana, he handed me a small gift, a 3 × 5 note card on which he wrote in pencil "7 Suggestions to Follow." It was a philosophy of life that he hoped would help me amount to something: "Johnny, try and live up to these things and you'll do all right." I came to call his gift the "7 Point Creed."

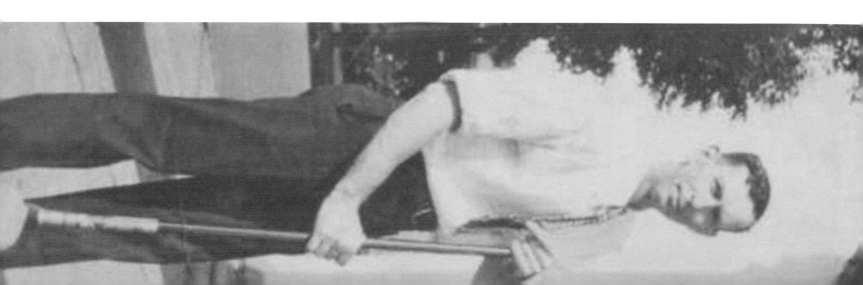

1. Be True to Yourself

Your integrity begins with you. If you are not true to yourself, how can you be true to others? It's impossible. Polonius tells his son Laertes in *Hamlet*:

"This above all, to thine own self be true, and it must follow as the night the day, thou cans't not then be false to any man." Dad believed there are no moral or ethical holidays. I agree.

I enlisted in the Navy without telling Nellie (that's our crew on the left during naval training exercises, with me standing farthest left). I knew I had to serve my country; I also knew that Nell, a wife and mother, would be extremely anxious and upset about what could happen. But like millions of other Americans, I did what I had to do.

"Dare to be Daniel/ Dare to stand alone/ Dare to have purpose firm/ Dare to make it known." —P. Bliss

2. Help Others

There is a mystical law of nature that says the three things we crave most in life—happiness, freedom, and peace of mind— are always attained by giving them to someone else. Your true happiness comes from giving, not getting. It's a basic precept of all great religions: the Golden Rule.

Coaching was my path to helping others. I received the Presidential Medal of Freedom by following my father's advice. I appreciate the honor, but the greater honor and joy was in the act itself—helping others.

"You cannot live a perfect day without doing something for another without thought of getting something in return."

—Mother Teresa

After WWII, I coached the Sycamores at Indiana State Teacher's College from 1946–1948.

Indiana State University Department of Athletics

3. Make Each Day Your Masterpiece

You cannot change yesterday, and a better tomorrow will be the result of what you do today. If you do your best, angels can do no better. And this present moment—right now—is when you have that opportunity.

This picture was taken moments after I coached my last game—UCLA's 92-85 victory over Kentucky in the 1975 NCAA final.

"Learn today as though you were to live forever; live today as if you were to die tomorrow."

ASUCLA Photography

That's me in 1969 with my two assistant coaches, Denny Crum and Gary Cunningham.

4. Drink Deeply from Good Books, Including *the* Good Book

There is no book that compares to the Bible, but Dad also read Shakespeare to his sons, and lots of poetry. I continued reading —the philosophers, biographies of great individuals, and other good literature. Dad reminded me often, "Johnny, you'll never learn a thing that you didn't learn from someone else." Good books help us do that.

When I graduated from Purdue, I was awarded the Big 10 medal for scholastic and athletic achievement. It made me proud, because Dad always stressed education. All four of his sons graduated and became teachers. He taught us to love good books.

5. Make Friendship a Fine Art

In spite of all that doctors know,
And their studies never end,
The best cure of all when spirits fall
Is a kind note from a friend.

—John Wooden

6. Build a Shelter against a Rainy Day

Dad was concerned with building a shelter from the storms of life, but equally important was building a spiritual shelter. Consider all things, not merely material things. He told me, "I don't know what the future holds, but I do know who holds the future."

That's my brother Billy (left), my brother Dan, my mother, me, and my brother Maurice taken at the time of my father's passing. During times of tragedy, there is no stronger shelter than that provided by family.

"Don't let making a living prevent you from making a life."

AP Images

Nell, Nan, Jim, and me on the couch of our home in Terre Haute, Indiana after I agreed to become the new head coach at UCLA, April 1948. Jimmy didn't look too happy about it.

7. Pray for Guidance, Count and Give Thanks for Your Blessings Each Day

You'll be much happier if you spend as much time thinking about your blessings as you do about your troubles.

In this regard, it is helpful to forget favors given and remember those received.

I pray thee, O God, that I may be beautiful within.

SOCRATES
13

"Four things a man must do/ If he would make his life more true/ To think without confusion clearly/ To love his fellow man sincerely/ To act from honest motives purely/ To trust in God and heaven securely." —Rev. Henry Van Dyke

Jimi Giannatti

Two Sets of Three's

For many years before Dad gave me his 7 Point Creed, he had drilled in my three brothers and me what he called the Two Sets of Three's. It was a simple guide to honesty and behavior:

1. Never lie.
2. Never cheat.
3. Never steal.

    1. Don't whine.
    2. Don't complain.
    3. Don't make excuses

Although I fall short of living up to my father's 7 Point Creed and Two Sets of Three's, I have found them to be meaningful in every phase of my life. I am much like the one who said, "I am not what I ought to be; not what I want to be; not what I am going to be; but I am thankful that I am better than what I used to be."

This picture of my three brothers and me with Dad is very significant: It's the only photo I have of the five of us together on the farm. Dad was the best man I ever knew, and the wisest. That's Billy on the left, then Dan, me, Maurice, and our father.

The person you are is the person your children become.
Show love and compassion, self-control and discipline;
seek knowledge and demonstrate good values.

South Bend Tribune

I am a teacher. Next to parenting itself, I believe that teaching is the most important profession in the world. Coaching is just another word for teaching; you may have a whistle, but you're still a teacher. I taught basketball, baseball, tennis, and English in South Bend, Indiana for nine years. That's me with the South Bend Central High School Bruins in the picture above.

At its highest level, teaching allows you to be a person who helps others become the best they can be. What can be more important—or fulfilling—than that?

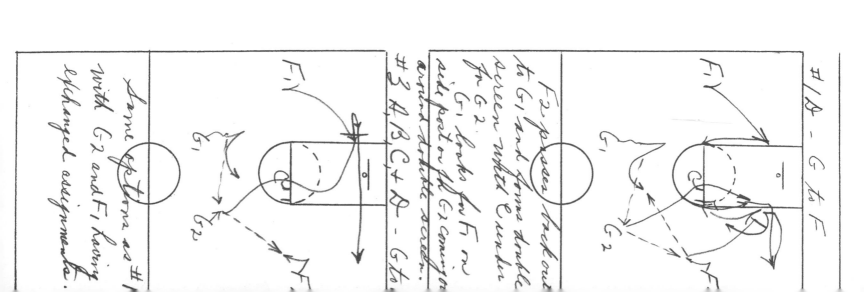

Mentors

The University of Chicago's Coach Amos Alonzo Stagg was congratulated by a local reporter after a good season back in the 1920s: "You did a great job!"

Coach Stagg paused, then replied, "I won't know how good a job I did for twenty years. That's when I'll see how my boys turned out."

The wins and losses matter: "How my boys turned out," mattered more to Coach Stagg. It mattered more to me, too.

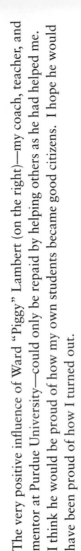

The very positive influence of Ward "Piggy" Lambert (on the right)—my coach, teacher, and mentor at Purdue University—could only be repaid by helping others as he had helped me. I think he would be proud of how my own students became good citizens. I hope he would have been proud of how I turned out.

"[A]s the coach—probably so the boy." Young people need good models more than they need critics. In the 1940s I wrote this reminder to myself of the responsibilities I assumed as a coach, English teacher, and mentor at South Bend Central High School in Indiana.

```
11. Reliability--The coach has a great responsibility and must
do more than just produce good teams.  He must teach and drill into
the boy this something we call sportsmanship.  Athletics should make
a boy a better citizen.  That ability to give and take and share the
responsibility of a good team with his mates should make a better
American.  But, don't forget, as the coach--probably so the boy.
```

No trophy has ever produced the deep satisfaction in me that the act of teaching produces. From the first day of my first week as a teacher and coach, I loved my job because of the great opportunity it gave me to change the lives of youngsters in a positive way. The bond between teacher and student is a sacred trust. I treated that bond with the utmost respect.

My own teachers—mentors—did the same for me. I relished the opportunity to do for others what they had done for me. They made me a better person. After my father, my teachers had the most profound impact on my life.

"No written word/ nor spoken plea/ Can teach our youth/ what they should be./ Nor all the books/ on all the shelves./ It's what the teachers/ are themselves." —John Wooden

Centerton School where Earl taught for seven years;

Earl Warriner became a lifelong friend, but before that he was the principal and my very first basketball coach at Centerton Grade School. "There are some things more important than winning a game," he cautioned me as I was sent to the bench. "No single player is more important than the team." I learned my lesson and taught that lesson to my own teams in later years: The star of the team is the team.

"What is success?"

Lawrence Shidler, my math teacher at Martinsville High (above), asked our class, "What is success?" He got me thinking that it wasn't just money, fame, or power. Perhaps there was something that mattered even more. It took me a few years to figure out what that was.

Sports

I've participated in sports throughout my life, both as a player and as a coach. The memories are wonderful—so many individuals who were dedicated, hard-working, and honorable. The bonds forged in the competitive arena last a lifetime. It was an environment that was so rewarding and fit my nature so well.

UCLA? Goodness gracious sakes alive, what can I say about that extraordinary time in my life! Nevertheless, I greatly enjoyed teaching at every step of the way. It was as fulfilling for me at the high school level as at the college level. Maybe more so. I was fortunate; I found the right profession for me—teaching.

Purdue University Archives and Special Collections

Purdue's "Piggy" Lambert (that's Coach Lambert on the right, me on the left) demonstrated the great bond between teacher and student—the sacred trust. He was a real taskmaster, but the welfare of his student-athletes was always paramount in Coach Lambert's mind. The team was extended family, and he cared about each one of us as a person. He was a model for what a coach should be, for what I wanted to be.

My high school coach, Glenn Curtis, inspired our team, the Martinsville Artesians, with poetry, but also showed me how to teach basketball—breaking it down into separate components, little parts, and perfecting the parts. We won the Indiana State High School Championship in 1927. (That's me seated in front of Coach Curtis.) The following year, with seconds left, I missed a free throw that could have won the championship again. I was team captain. That loss still hurts, but I was very proud of my effort before and during the game. In the locker room afterward, everyone was depressed, crying, or getting ready to cry. Everyone except me. I took pride in my effort.

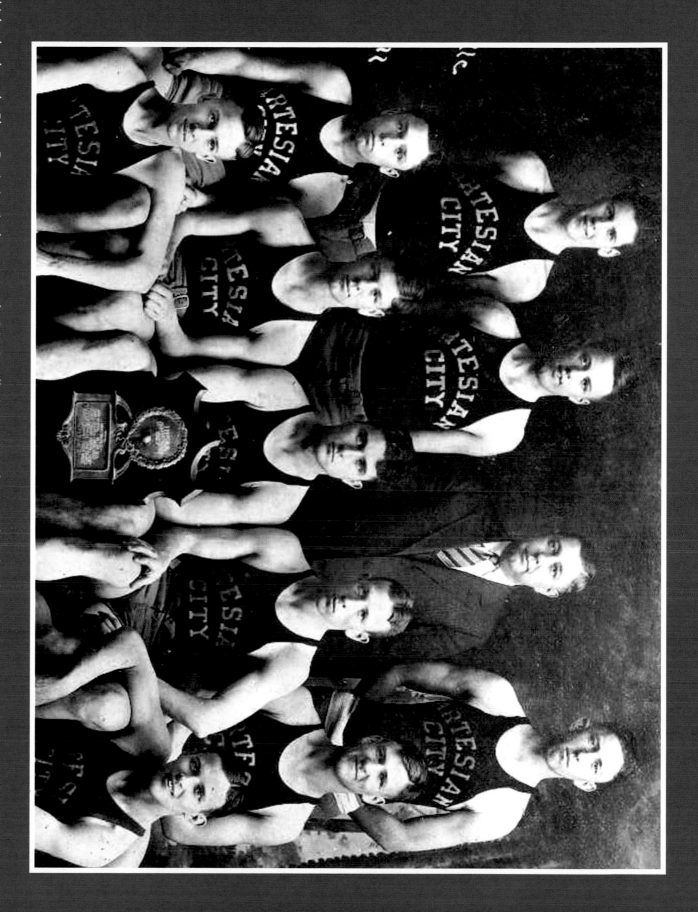

This picture of me was in Nellie's high school yearbook, *The Artesian*. She did a little "decorating" on my picture.

I was thirty-one years old, coaching at South Bend Central High when this photograph was taken—diagramming a play for an upcoming tournament game in Hammond, Indiana.

JIM FARNER.   EDDIE EHLERS.   JOHN WOODEN.   HARVEY MARTENS.

"The journey is better than the inn." —Cervantes

(Above) That's me in the white jersey getting a jump ball during a 1944 Navy recreational game. (Right) Ten years later, a publicity photo during the 1954 season. The woman in the picture was a Bruin booster.

UCLA
Basketball
1953-54
SCHEDULE

16 Big Home Games.

December 4	ALUMNI ALL - STARS
December 5	WEST TEXAS STATE
December 11, 12	ARIZONA
December 26, 28	OREGON

Dec. 30 - IOWA vs. UCLA, MICH. STATE vs. USC
Dec. 31 - IOWA vs. USC, MICH. STATE vs. UCLA

January 29 COLLEGE OF PACIFIC
January 30 PEPPERDINE
February 5, 6 STANFORD
February 12, 13 SOUTHERN CALIFORNIA
February 26, 27

UCLA MEN'S GYM

CALL ASUCLA
VARSITY TICKET OFFICE

If I had done my job effectively as a teacher during the week, I felt I could virtually go up in the stands and watch the team compete. They should know what to do without me telling them.

Nevertheless, since I was on the bench, I offered direction when I felt it necessary.

I was intense but never uncontrolled in the huddle. No screaming, no profanity. That short period of time was valuable. I didn't want emotions to spill over and spoil the opportunity. Not just in a huddle, but in life, I value self-control highly. (Right) The 1964 NCAA Championship game against Duke. That's Ducky Drake, our trainer, offering a little citrus nourishment while I make a point. (Above) A lighter moment on the bench.

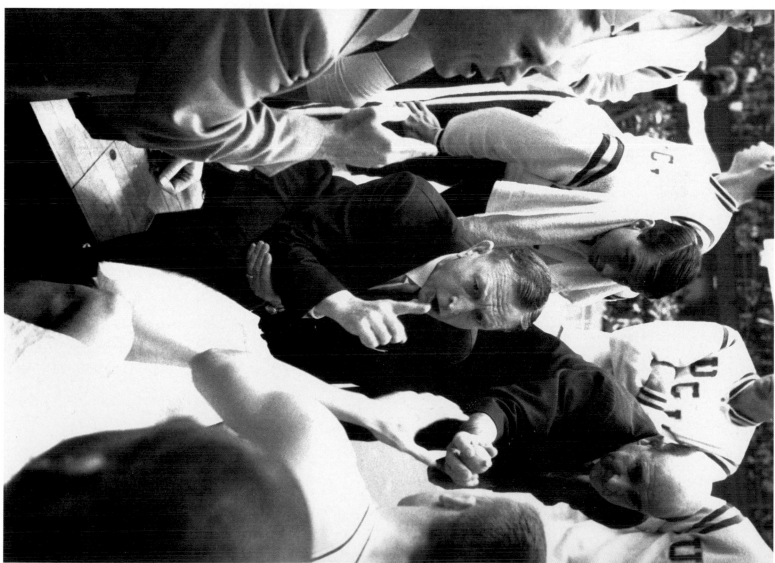

Sports Illustrated/Getty Images

I instructed players to control their emotions after a big victory: "Let the fans and alumni make fools of themselves. Don't you do it." I wanted student-athletes to behave in a sportsmanlike manner regardless of the outcome: "When you leave the arena, a bystander shouldn't be able to tell by your demeanor whether you won or lost."

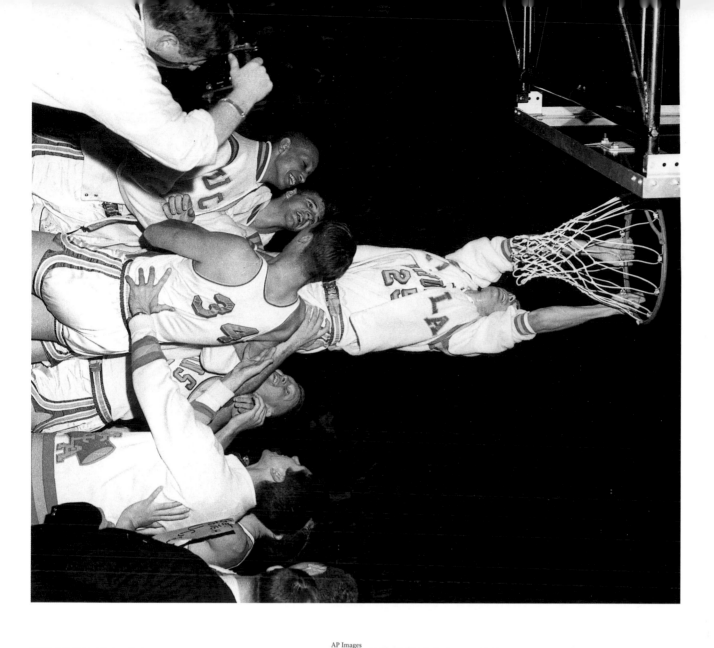

AP Images

Louisville's coach, Denny Crum, and I shake hands after our semifinal game for the national championship on March 29, 1975, in San Diego. It was bittersweet for me—as close to a perfect game as I'd ever participated in, for both teams. It went to overtime; UCLA eventually won, 75–74. I was pleased that UCLA came out on top, but I sincerely felt bad for Denny, who had been a hard-working player for us at UCLA in 1958 and 1959, and later had been an exceptional assistant coach with us in 1969, 1970, 1971, years that produced three national championships. If we'd called the game a draw after regulation play, I would have been fine with that. No problem at all. Denny later coached Louisville to two March Madness national championships, which pleased me very much.

They called it the Game of the Century—January 20, 1968. It was played in the vast Houston Astrodome. I didn't like the idea because I thought the size of it all turned the event into a show business spectacle. It wasn't up to me to decide, however. UCLA was ranked #1; Houston #2. We lost, in part because Houston's Elvin Hayes played very well, in part because Lewis Alcindor had severely limited vision in his left eye because of an injury. He made no complaint. Lewis did, however, tape this cover of *Sports Illustrated* to his locker. Eight weeks later we faced Houston in the semifinals of March Madness. The Bruins outscored Houston 101-69. Lewis's left eye was back to normal. I considered us successful in both games.

"There is no such thing as an overachiever. We are all underachievers to varying degrees."

ASUCLA Photography

Trophies are not success, nor does possessing them necessarily mean you are a success. Success is measured by the quality of effort you put forth to do your best. And only you know if you have accomplished that. Then if everything goes well, you may get a trophy; often you don't. You're still a success in my way of thinking. The score cannot make you a loser when you have given it your best effort.

Life

Basketball or any other sport can be great fun to play and very entertaining to watch. However, it offers something more important. The lessons it provides—taught properly—apply directly to life. Many of those lessons are usually taught first by a good mother and father, but sports can help make them stick and add a few more.

Dad said, "Son, don't ever think you're better than somebody else, but never forget you're just as good as anybody. No better, but just as good."

That's how he taught me about equality. Blacks, whites, men, women—everybody equal. He was pretty advanced.

When a committee in 1947 invited our Indiana State Sycamores to a big playoff tournament in Kansas City but told me I couldn't bring Clarence Walker along, I refused to go. The next year I turned them down again. The tournament committee relented. Clarence broke the color barrier in whites-only tournaments.

I stood up for Clarence, but Clarence also had to stand up for himself. And he did.

Southern Indiana was a hotbed of racism when Dad was growing up. Somehow he walked a higher road and took my brothers and me with him.

The Queens Borough Public Library—New York Herald Tribune

Indiana State

The committee asked that I leave #32 behind. How could I?

Lewis Alcindor, Jr., came to UCLA with a clear understanding that race was not an issue with our basketball team (or with our university). As one of his teammates said, "Coach Wooden doesn't see color." It was a compliment to my dad.

"Everybody's equal. That's what Dad taught my brothers and me."

This poem I used as a guide in raising my son and daughter, Jim and Nan, and also in teaching, coaching, and mentoring students and student-athletes for many decades.

"It is one of the most

beautiful compensations

of this life that no person

can sincerely help another

without helping himself."

—Ralph Waldo Emerson

A Little Fellow Follows Me

A careful man I want to be.
A little fellow follows me;
I do not dare to go astray,
For fear he'll go the self-same way.

I cannot once escape his eyes,
Whate'er he sees me do, he tries;
Like me he says he's going to be,
The little chap who follows me.

He thinks that I am good and fine,
Believes in every word of mine;
The base in me he must not see,
The little chap who follows me.

I must remember as I go,
Through summer's sun and winter's snow;
I am building for the years to be
That little chap who follows me.

THE GROLIER SOCIETY, INC.

The original of this was presented to me in 1936 upon the birth of my son and has been kept nearby since then. John Wooden, UCLA

Teacher and student, 1973.

Bill Walton was not so "little," but he was a "chap who followed me."

Student and teacher, 2010.

Bill's not the only "little fellow" who grew up and became a person I'm proud to know. There isn't a student-athlete I taught who wouldn't be welcome in my home. In the years since they graduated, I've been proud of all those I taught. They turned out to be fine people: productive members of our society, good citizens. Good Americans.

Nowadays they teach me a thing or two; now I'm often the student and the helping hand comes from them. I'm proud of the role I played in their lives and grateful for the role they play in mine.

Basketball is of little importance compared to the rest of the life that we live.

Lewis gives me an assist.

In life there are few goals more worthwhile and satisfying than helping others. Teachers, coaches, mentors, and leaders have that wonderful opportunity. It is an opportunity exceeded only by that of being a parent. All are based on giving—not the material things, but rather love, support, knowledge, guidance, kindness, discipline, and even wisdom such as my father and mother offered my brothers and me. Ralph Waldo Emerson said it well: "Material things are not gifts but apologies for gifts. The only true gift is a portion of thyself."

1973: Greg Lee listens to a teacher—a most valuable asset both on and off the court.

Be quick, but don't hurry.

BEYOND THE BASKETBALL

Beyond the grand Pavilion,
Where Bruin banners span,
Beyond the accolades, I learned
To be a champion man.

Far beyond material,
Or book on any shelf,
Beyond the break, the pass or play,
I learned about myself.

Beyond the fundamentals,
Or how to work the task,
Beyond the "how," I learned the "why"
And learned to think and ask.

Beyond the Bruin uniform,
Beyond the Blue and Gold,
I gained a pride in who I am,
That lasts until I'm old.

And far beyond instruction,
Beyond the hardwood class,
Beyond the game and all the tests,
Beyond the fail or pass,

The Teacher loved me, so he coached
Beyond gymnasium wall.
I thank my God, The Teacher taught,
Beyond the basketball.

—Swen Nater, UCLA Men's Basketball, 1971–1973,
in honor of Coach Wooden

I will not like you all the same, but I will love you all the same. Each one of you will receive the treatment you earn and deserve.

That's my father, my older brother Maurice, me, my mother, and my younger brother Dan up in front (Billy hadn't arrived yet).

Sunday morning many years ago, I was in church when the pastor told the congregation that our priorities should be in this order: faith, family, and friends. As much as I wanted to abide by the pastor's suggestion, I couldn't. For me the priorities have always been like this: family, faith, and friends.

Family is first for me. I can't help it, and I hope the Good Lord forgives me. Nevertheless, faith has always been strong in my life. And, of course, so are friends. Family, faith, and friends: if you've got that, you've got pretty much everything regardless of the order.

Family

Nellie Riley is the only girl I ever loved. We were sweethearts for nearly sixty years —married for fifty-three of them. When our children came along, Nancy and Jim, they brought us happiness and more love—and then grandchildren and even more love!

Abraham Lincoln said, "The best thing a man can do for his children is to love their mother." Well, I did. A lot. My reward? A lifetime of love in return.

My great-grandson, Cam, is a special child of God.

He has created so much love in the lives of others,

especially his family. He is a blessing to me.

Cori, my very first great-grandchild, just got married.

I hope to be around long enough to give my very

first great-great-grandchild a great big hug!

We were fortunate enough to share our love with our children, grandchildren, and great-grandchildren. Here I am with my daughter, Nan, and her family.

And here's my son, Jim, and his family.

Faith

I am a Christian. Over our years together, Nellie and I found the greatest strength and hope in our faith. We shared it with our children, and they with their children. But I also respect those whose faith is different from mine.

Thus, I was not particularly concerned with what religious beliefs my student-athletes held, although I did want them to believe in something because it can make you a better person. I told them, "Have a faith, a religion, and know why you believe in it. Stand up for those beliefs, but respect the rights of others to believe in their own faith."

What kind of a person has no creed, no faith, no moral compass guiding them? What kind of person forces their faith on others?

At the core of all great religions, in one form or another, is the exhortation to love our fellow man. Whether you're a Christian, Jew, Buddhist, or Muslim, it's important to always keep that in mind. Too many forget this basic tenet of their faith.

In 1943, when I was entering the Navy, my pastor gave me a little silver cross to carry with me. I still have it and, in fact, held it in my hand for every single game I ever coached when I returned from the service—not for good luck, not to help us win, but to remind me of who I am. When my final day arrives, if you search my pocket you will find that little silver cross. It served me well. I hope I served it equally well.

Friends

Friends are a blessing, and I have been greatly blessed. While those I taught became part of my extended family, they also were my friends, as were so many others I met along the way.

Friendship is a two-way street. Go more than halfway. Webster's dictionary says friendship includes "mutual esteem, respect, and devotion." Remember, we are judged by the friends we have made. Don't take friendship for granted. Good friends are part of life's treasure.

Many of the student-athletes I coached got together for a 2003 reunion at Pauley Pavilion to commemorate the naming of the court we once played on as "The Nell & John Wooden Court." I am so proud of how they turned out—doctors, dentists, preachers, businessmen, and more. I am so proud that they got their education. And used it.

My teaching has allowed me to make so many new friends—of all ages.

It is never too soon to show your love because you never know when it'll be too late. My son, Jim, agrees.

This may surprise you: My father never taught me a thing about playing basketball. What he taught my brothers and me was more valuable:

"Johnny, don't worry about being better than somebody else, but never cease trying to be the best you can be. You have control over that, not the other."

He was educating me to judge success in basketball, school, and ultimately life by how hard I worked to fulfill my potential, however great or small it might be in different areas. Years later, I remembered his advice.

When I entered the teaching and coaching profession at Dayton High School in Kentucky, I found out there were people who judged my success as an English teacher solely on my ability to turn out "A" students and my success as a basketball coach by the winning percentage of my teams. So many other factors influence these things that such criteria are grossly invalid and unfair.

ASUCLA Photography

Therefore, I began searching for some method, at least for my students and me, that might be a more realistic and honest appraisal of success —one that would prize above all the quality of your effort rather than how you stacked up against somebody else.

I wanted a definition of success reflecting my dad's advice about working hard—ceaselessly—to reach my potential. A little poem I read while I was searching for an answer put things very clearly:

At God's footstool, to confess,

A poor soul knelt and bowed his head.

"I failed," he cried. The Master said,

"Thou didst thy best.

That is success."

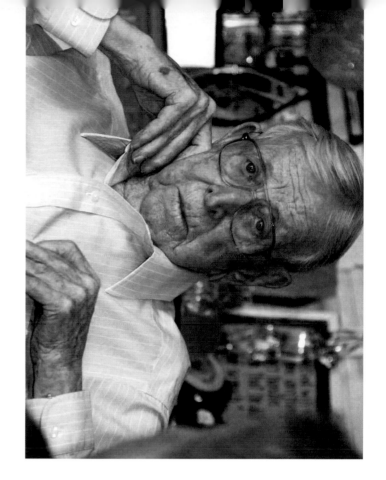

After considerable reflection, I coined my own definition in 1932:

Success is peace of mind, which is a direct result of self-satisfaction in knowing you made the effort to become the best you are capable of becoming.

I believe that is the highest level of success. All that comes from that effort, the "rewards," are a by-product. I've basically stayed with that definition ever since.

I soon realized, however, that I owed it to my students to help them understand what they must do to achieve success. The Pyramid of Success contains the fifteen personal qualities I chose as prerequisites for success as I define it.

PYRAMID OF SUCCESS

THE ART OF

success

John Wooden, Head Coach

SUCCESS

FAITH

PATIENCE

COMPETITIVE GREATNESS
Be at your best when your best is needed. Welcome the hard battle.

POISE
Be yourself. No posing or pretense; be at ease in any situation.

CONFIDENCE
You must earn the right to be proud and confident. Failing to prepare is preparing to fail.

CONDITION
Mental, moral, and physical ability may get you to the top, but it takes character to stay there.

SKILL
Know your stuff! Be prepared. Little things make big things happen.

TEAM SPIRIT
Be eager to sacrifice personal interests or glory for the welfare of all. The team comes first.

SELF-CONTROL
Control emotion or emotion will control you; discipline yourself so others won't need to.

ALERTNESS
Pay attention! Don't get caught napping. Failure's companion is complacency.

INITIATIVE
Failure to act is often the biggest failure of all. Be quick, but don't hurry.

INTENTNESS
Goals achieved with little effort are seldom worthwhile or long-lasting. Rest, if necessary; never quit.

INDUSTRIOUSNESS
There is no trick, no easy way. Very hard work precedes success.

FRIENDSHIP
Strive to be a good friend, and you will be surrounded by good friends.

LOYALTY
Be true to yourself— and to others.

COOPERATION
Be more concerned with finding the best way than with having it your way.

ENTHUSIASM
Your enthusiasm and energy —bubbling over—transform "work" into a joyous and irresistible endeavor.

Love is the basis for everything I do.

Many years later, parents began asking me to put my ideas about success and the Pyramid into a form that their children could understand. Inch and Miles, the stars of my children's book, have helped youngsters across America better understand what I teach. School Specialty, the folks who take Inch and Miles into classrooms, asked me if I had ever thought about changing my Pyramid in any manner.

I replied, "No, except for one thing. I wish I had included the word 'Love' somewhere. Love is the basis for everything I do." The next thing I knew, they granted me my wish!

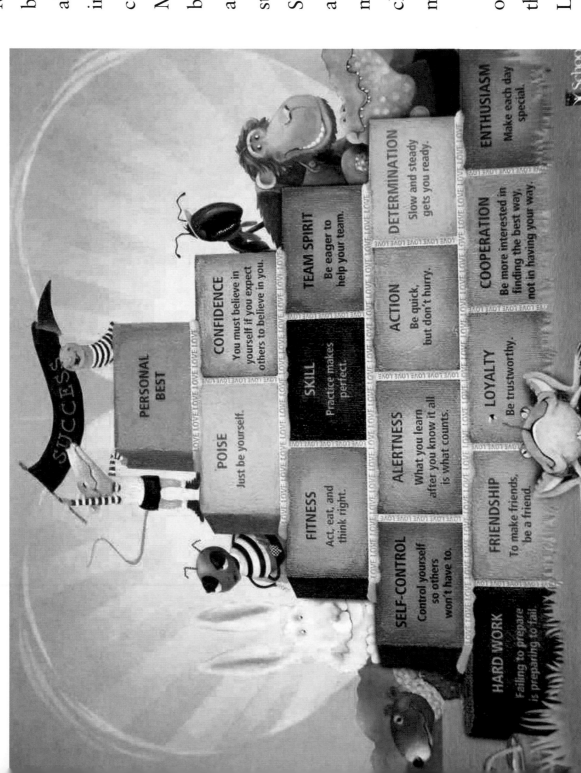

Inch and Miles atop my Pyramid that's filled with love.

My Sportsmanship Pledge for Youngsters

When I gave my Sportsmanship Pledge to my great-grandson, he looked a bit skeptical, but not as skeptical as Bill Walton when he took the Pledge.

The "whistle" doesn't teach. The leader who blows the whistle teaches. Unless, of course, it's a magic whistle such as the one Inch and Miles use when they go on a journey to find Success.

I'll be a good sport
    when I win or I lose.

No whining, complaining,
    or making excuse.

I'll always keep trying
    one hundred percent

To give my best effort
    on every event.

This sportsmanship pledge
    will bring out my best.

Coach Wooden has taught me
    to be a success!

Which is the greatest team I ever coached? There is no such as thing as a "greatest team" in my mind, nor a greatest player. In my view, greatness can be attained by each one of us when we make our finest effort to become the best we are capable of becoming.

1948-1949

No championship, but an authentic success: my first ever team at UCLA. These boys made the most of what they had—100 percent—and in so doing achieved success.

In my den, among the books and papers and memorabilia, is a Pyramid of Success composed of pictures of the ten UCLA teams that won men's national basketball championships. I was going to hang the photos in a straight line, but Nell had a better plan—a pyramid of pictures.

I don't look for "greatest." I seek greatness.

And it is available to each one of us.

I was asked, "John, do you think it's harder to get to the top or stay on top?" I replied,

"I believe it's much easier to stay on top because once you're there all the talent comes knocking."

God didn't make us all equal in ability; we're not equal as far as size or appearance. We don't all have the same advantages as others, but we are all equal as far as having the same opportunity to make the most of what we have—whatever that may be.

When you give yourself fully to that effort, whatever your circumstance or situation—good, bad, or otherwise—you have done all you can do. That is success. And when you do so, only you really know. That's what my father told me; it's what I told my students: Only you truly know if you are a success.

The Pyramid, hopefully, is a guide to attaining it.

Judy Olian, dean of the UCLA Anderson School of Management, helped establish the John Wooden Global Leadership Award as part of its John Wooden Leadership Program. Its purpose is to share my ideas on leadership with the leaders of the future. In the bottom photo, Dean Olian and I are joined by Howard Schultz, CEO of Starbucks (seated, left) and Andy Serwer, managing editor of *Fortune* magazine. Mr. Schultz was the first recipient of the John Wooden Global Leadership Award.

January 19, 1974: In twenty-one seconds, our eighty-eight-game winning streak would come to an end

I want to be clear
about something:
Winning or losing matters.

I want to be clear about something: Winning or losing matters. Why else would we keep score? When you win, it usually feels good. Losing hurts, and it should. But my belief is that winning and losing are a by-product, offshoot, consequence of something more important. That's why in my early years of teaching, I sought to figure out what that "something" was.

My definition of success, my concept of what constitutes "greatness" in an individual or a team and how to achieve those lofty goals, is put in perspective with a simple directive:

Do not judge yourself by what you have achieved but rather by what you could and should have achieved given your potential—if you'd never ceased trying to be the best you could be.

Perfection is a goal that can never be reached, but it must be your objective. Work ceaselessly to improve. Remember, the uphill climb is slow; the downhill road is fast. The quality of your effort counts most.

REFLECTIONS ON A JOURNEY

It's been a long time since this young boy left the farm. But the farm—and what I learned there—never left the young boy. As I grew older, time seemed to go by faster and faster. I guess that's true for most of us. One day I turned around and looked back, and what did I see? Not just years, but decades and decades and decades. How did all that time go by so fast? Where is it? My photographs help me see the journey but do little to explain how it can go by so quickly—in the blink of an eye. Some call it the game of life. Although I was involved in lots of games over the years, I never believed life is just a game.

Pull up my socks, tap my assistant coach on the knee, then turn and find Nellie in the stands and give her an "A-OK" sign. This was my pre-game ritual, which started —the finding Nellie in the stands part of it—when I was playing guard at Martinsville High, and held for almost fifty years.

Nellie loved being at my games whether I was a player or coach. In her heart, however, she valued something else much more, namely, that I would be a good husband and father. She had her priorities in order. We had the same priorities.

My life has taken me places I could never have imagined when I was a youngster. It also has offered up more than its share of entertaining moments along the way.

Converse asked me to help design a new basketball sneaker. I thought I came up with a winner—more room for toes, lighter, and good looking. Apparently, they weren't as good looking as I thought, and if you stopped quickly, you might skid. That was my last attempt to design basketball equipment!

A painting by Jeff Wong was part of a cover for *Sports Illustrated*. Nellie wasn't here to see this particular version of her husband, but she would have chuckled at it as much I did. More, in fact.

My Bill Walton mask pales in comparison to Bill Walton except in one important way: The mask doesn't talk all the time. That's why I'm fond of wearing the Bill Walton mask occasionally—silence!

Even if the request for an autograph came from an individual who looked a little unusual, I was happy to oblige. I told players if a fan asks you for an autograph, sign it. They are paying you an honor; treat them with respect. Some didn't agree with me, but they were wrong.

Steve Jamison and I have enjoyed working together for over fifteen years because it's productive and it's fun. There's a lesson there. The very first blocks that I selected for the Pyramid of Success were Industriousness and Enthusiasm. When your work is no more than a grind, you cannot perform up to your highest level. A little fun is part of Enthusiasm.

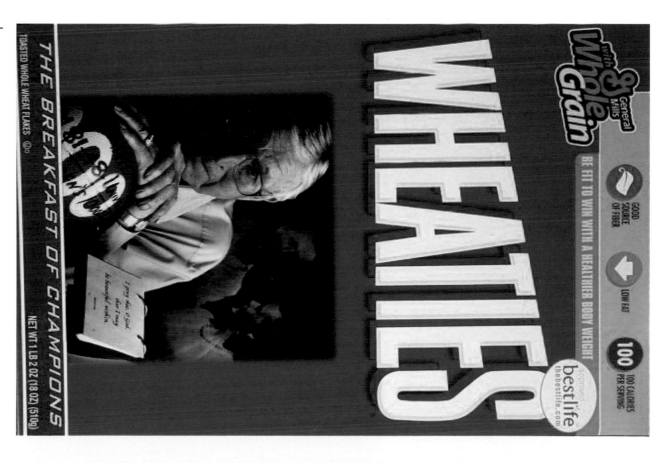

A box of Wheaties with my picture on it made me smile, because, when I was growing up, Wheaties hadn't been invented yet. Mother cooked oatmeal every morning along with the eggs and bacon and homemade bread with homemade blackberry jam. She was feeding four hungry sons and their dad. Mom would have loved a box of cereal to help her out. Especially if it had a picture of one of her sons on it!

I have a fondness for maxims because they convey so much with so little. Here are four that I use frequently and effectively:

1. Do not mistake activity for achievement.

2. Things work out best for those who make the best of the way things work out.

3. A player who makes the team great is better than a great player.

4. The best way to improve the team is to improve yourself.

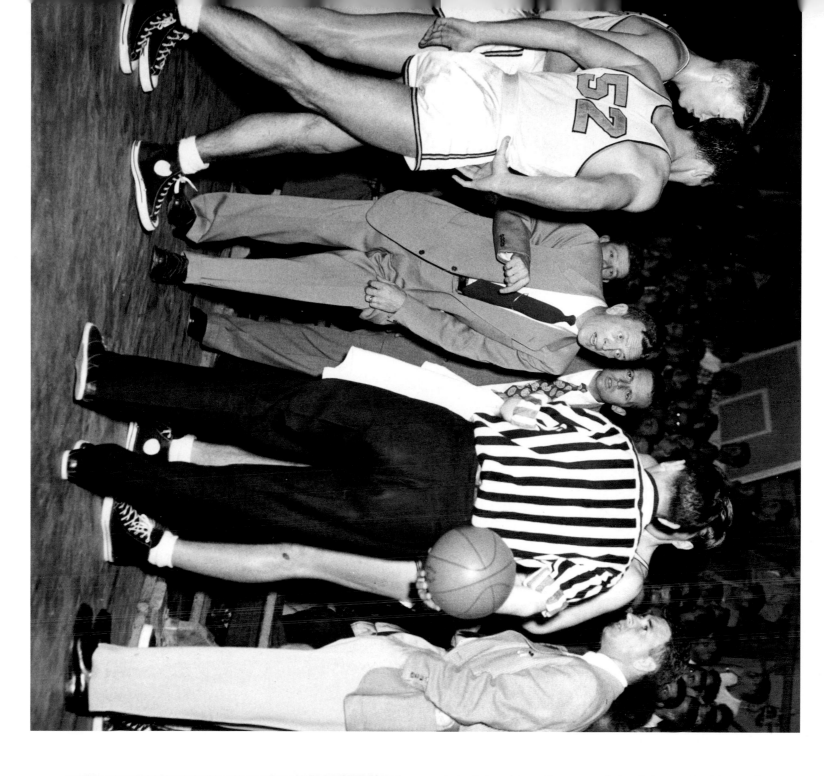

AP Images

The referee, Lou Stringer, made a call under the basket that I thought was just terrible. As he ran past our bench, I shouted, "Lou, that was a horrible call you made—just horrible!" He winked and yelled back, "John, they loved it at the other end!"

The result of desire is

often desired results.

This was the first

basketball court

I ever played on.

It was dirt.

And it was beautiful.

Sports Illustrated/Getty Images

My final ten years of coaching were done at UCLA's beautiful state-of-the-art Pauley Pavilion, which offered an extraordinary facility for my teaching. But whether it was a dirt court like the one I grew up playing on (above right), Pauley Pavilion, or the good schools in between, I was unceasing in the effort to do my best. When you have done that, you have done everything. When you have done less, you have done nothing.

For all of us there should be joy in the journey, but we must also know it will bring its share of strife, struggle, and frustration. How you deal with it determines how it deals with you.

This is a ticket for my final game as a teacher of basketball at UCLA—the 1975 national championship with Kentucky. However, it was not a ticket to my retirement from teaching. Since that day in March, I have continued trying to help others in ways that others—my parents, teachers, mentors—helped me. It brings the greatest satisfaction. Giving of yourself, as Ralph Waldo Emerson said, is the greatest gift of all. What he didn't say is that it's also the most joyous and rewarding gift to give.

Disappointment is part of the process. If you're not resilient, you will not last—you will break.

It has been a century for me—a wonderful journey—filled with so many people I love and respect and have learned from. And, because I've been around so long, folks occasionally ask, "Coach Wooden, are you afraid of dying?" My answer? "No. Not at all. When the time comes, I know I'll be with Nellie again, and that will be a glorious day for us."

I also remember what Socrates said when his jailers—cruel, mocking men—asked why he was not preparing himself for his imminent death by poisoning. He said quietly and calmly, "I have prepared myself for death all my life by the life I've lived." His example is one we should keep in mind during our own time here on earth. I've tried to do that, and now, like him, death has no fear for me.

Once I was afraid of dying,
Terrified of ever-lying,
Petrified of leaving family, home and friends.
Thoughts of absence from my dear ones,
Drew a melancholy tear once,
And a lonely, dreadful fear of when life ends.

But those days are long behind me;
Fear of leaving does not bind me,
And departure does not host a single care.
Peace does comfort as I ponder,
Reunion in the Yonder,
With my dearest who are waiting over there.

—Swen Nater, inspired by Coach Wooden

As we say goodbye for now, I would like to remind you of my dad's advice. His wisdom still amazes me; his teaching still guides me. So many things he taught are valuable, but one of the most important is contained in his 7 Point Creed: "Make each day your masterpiece."

For the better part of a century I have attempted to do that. To whatever degree I have succeeded, I thank Dad. When he spoke, I listened. Lucky for me.

John Wooden

One last place setting: June 5, 2010,

Coach's reserved table at VIP's Café, Tarzana, CA.